The
SECRET
to HEALING
AND FINDING COMFORT

The
SECRET
to HEALING
AND FINDING COMFORT

RECOVERING FROM
GRIEF WITH SOUL FOOD
(FOOD FOR THE SOUL)

E. Talley Washington

iUniverse

THE SECRET TO HEALING AND FINDING COMFORT
RECOVERING FROM GRIEF WITH SOUL FOOD
(FOOD FOR THE SOUL)

iUniverse books may be ordered through booksellers or by contacting:

iUniverse
1663 Liberty Drive
Bloomington, IN 47403
www.iuniverse.com
1-800-Authors (1-800-288-4677)

ISBN: 978-1-4917-7010-8 (sc)
ISBN: 978-1-4917-7086-3 (e)

Library of Congress Control Number: 2015909784

Print information available on the last page.

iUniverse rev. date: 01/26/2016

To my child, Precious,
my grandchildren,
my cousins, family, and
friends who knew my mom.
To those who were the objects of her love and affection,
and to all those who sat and ate at the table of
Lillian Martin Talley.

"Honor thy father and thy mother …"

To those who have loved and lost.
To everyone who knows the value and secret in the
healing properties of good food with good company.

To all who have cried and grieved
over the death of a loved one.

CONTENTS

CONTENTS

INTRODUCTION

It was never my intention to write a book or sell my mother's recipes. This book is a result of grief work—my intense work at "getting over" the death of my mother. While I was getting over her absence, I discovered—bitterly, slowly—that recovering from the loss of a loved one requires work. Just as losing weight or inches requires exercise, regaining your composure or spiritual equilibrium after a loss requires reflection, appreciation, thanksgiving, and adjusting to a new life without the person or situation you had before.

Originally this was a thirty-page collection of my mother's recipes, created for my daughter as a Mother's Day gift. Two months after I gave Precious her book, I found my mother's sweet-potato recipes and just had to have them in the book. Then a friend asked, "Are you sure *all* these things are okay? I mean, have you tried each recipe?" Well, my friend, that is when the adventure began!

After I tried each recipe, I would remember an incident involving my mother, relive a lively conversation between us, or laugh at a joke she shared. By the time I cooked the last dish, I was a fatter, happier person who was finally whole and well adjusted. During the months that I cooked and ate what she had cooked so well, I reflected on many things, appreciated my mom and her wisdom, and finally was grateful for all of it. Some things in my mother's past and mine are not so pretty, yet I have grown to appreciate all of that. I am thankful for the rough times and the peaceful times. The two make a great whole!

I encourage anyone who is struggling with grief to take all the time you need to work it out. What is grief? Grief is your pain, your reaction to a loss—any loss. If something or someone has been removed from your life, then you have experienced a loss and you probably grieved. Whether the loss is a person, a pet, an object, a job, good health, finances, teeth, looks, a situation you enjoyed, if you no longer have it and it was not your choice to be without, whatever is gone represents a loss. Loss hurts; grief ensues.

Now that I am healed and whole, I can share my mother and her great dishes with you.

After each recipe was tested, I revised my collection and added newly found recipes, such as the sweet-potato collection.

Let me add a tiny warning or a disclaimer: These are not quick and easy methods of cooking or meal planning. I and the editorial department have included directions to explain and simplify each recipe. Most recipes use real food that require a prolonged cooking time; there are no instant items in this collection, no use of the microwave or the food processor. It is common knowledge that the internet is full of quick and easy preparations and the cable network have a variety of shows that give instruction on preparing a meal in 30 minutes. This not that kind of book. This is not a Cook Book, but there are recipes inside. This is not a journal, but there is space inside for you to write down your thoughts. Actually this is my gift to anyone who is extremely sad and need a way to work out their grief. Everything can be done in the privacy of one's home, particularly the kitchen. The man or woman that finds solace in slicing carrots or chopping onions may find comfort during the preparations and assignments. I truly hope that the person that does not know their way around a kitchen will find a pearl in a recipe, a story, a scripture or an exercise.

I want you to meet the woman who inspired The Secret to Healing and Finding Comfort.

If I'd brought you to meet my mother, she would have wanted to have some food available, and the three of us would eat a little something as we became acquainted. So we will begin our meeting with a light snack of Shrimp Balls, crackers, and a drink.

> **Shrimp Balls**
> 2 lbs. raw shrimp, cleaned, deveined, and cut into small pieces
> 1 egg
> 1 medium potato, boiled and finely mashed
> ½ c. green onions
> ½ c. fresh parsley
> 1 medium onion
> dash cayenne pepper and salt to taste
> about 2 c. oil for frying
> a fry pot or skillet for frying
> about a cup of flour

Mix shrimp, egg, and mashed potato in a bowl. Clean and finely chop onions and parsley. Taste the mixture and add salt and/or cayenne pepper to your liking. Mix well. Add flour to hold mixture together. Shape into balls or cakes. Add more flour as needed. Drop into hot oil and fry both sides until golden brown. Drain on paper towels. Shrimp Balls are served with fancy little crackers.

Depending on the time of day, we would have either ice-cold lemonade or a cup of coffee. We like lemonade; it is such a quick thing to make and it goes with everything.

Lemonade
6-8 fresh lemons
About a cup of sugar* or to your taste
1 can of ginger ale
or try agave juice instead and avoid the coma

Squeeze all the lemons and grate the rind of one lemon. Put the sugar in the bottom of a one-quart pitcher. Add the lemon juice, the grated rind and all the pulp. Add the ginger ale and water until the pitcher is full. (If you don't like ginger ale, don't use it; we like ginger ale in our lemonade and punches.) STIR! Pour over ice. No matter how cold your lemonade, pour this stuff over ice so you don't go into a sugar coma. Serve in a tall glass. To make it look cute, add fresh mint.

Momma likes to talk, so sip your sugar-lemon concoction *slowly*, because she will refill your glass every time it gets empty.

Meet Lillian. She loved to eat and she loved to cook. She cooked what she ate, and I ate what she cooked. She was a no-nonsense, precise person. If her recipe called for a quarter teaspoon of salt, that is what you used and not a grain more! She was stern and to the point; she said what she meant and meant what she said. You might not have liked her; the timid and the shy rarely did. Many feared her or feared what she might say out loud in public.

This is how she taught me to cook: she dictated the way to prepare a particular dish, and I was supposed to write down the directions.

I tried, but I could never keep up with the papers I wrote on. So she gave me a pack of three-by-five-inch cards to write the directions on and a metal box to keep them in. Soon I had my very own "cook box." As I grew up, my cook box grew with more and more recipes. By the time I was a teenager, I had a large collection of recipes in my little green box, both from my mother and from my own findings. My uncle, a chef, began sharing his recipes with me and they were stored in the box too. By my junior year in high school I was a younger version of my mother in the kitchen.

When I became an adult, my mother gave me a beautiful pink scrolled-tin box full of her original recipes—recipes that had been tried, tested, cooked, and served several times. Since I cooked quite often at my mother's house, I kept the pink box there. When Momma left her house and this earth, the pretty pink tin box full of her original recipes mysteriously disappeared. After the final cleaning of her house, when I failed to find the pink box, I sadly returned to my home with a curious wooden box that had a roll-back lid. I stored that box on a high shelf in my kitchen along with several cookbooks, and left it to gather dust for years.

One day, out of sheer boredom, I pulled the wooden box down and looked inside. It was full of three-by-five cards with all kinds of advice, cooking tips, and recipes for anything and everything edible! Like a child with a newfound treasure box, I closed my eyes and pulled a card, vowing to cook whatever I ended up with. The first card I pulled sent me shopping for a mysterious ingredient that I had not been introduced to before: barley! The barley recipe is included in the "Rainy-Day Sunshine" chapter of this book.

This book contains only a fraction of the collection of recipes found in the wooden box. Some were in her handwriting; others were the backs of food boxes or labels from cans. Most are reproductions from other sources—few, if any are original—but they are all secrets to a good dish or meal.

I share with you my mom, Lillian, and her secret to providing comfort and love: her treasured recipes, the most-used recipes in the box. Also included here are a few secrets of my own, inspired by my mother.

A good example is my mother's prized recipe for Stuffed Cabbage, her most-frequently cooked dish. We had it often while I was growing up. It held a surprise within each cabbage roll, for Momma would tuck last week's leftovers into each one. The leftovers inside make this dish even tastier and more fun—better than the directions here. There is definitely room for creativity!

Stuffed Cabbage

Makes 10–12 servings—enough to fill you and to share with someone else.

1 3-lb. head green cabbage
¼ c. butter or margarine, divided
1 small onion, chopped
1 lb. lean ground beef
1½ lb. lean ground pork
1½ c. cooked long-grain rice
1 tsp. salt
¼ tsp. freshly ground black pepper
3½ c. beef broth, can or fresh
1 6-oz. can tomato paste
2 Tbsp. all-purpose flour

With a sharp knife, remove core from cabbage. Carefully remove and discard wilted or decayed outer leaves. In a large saucepan, boil enough salted water to cover cabbage. Immerse cabbage in boiling water. Cover and cook over medium-high heat for 5–7 minutes. With a fork or tongs, gently remove leaves as they become tender. Drain well; cool.

Preheat oven to 325°F. Melt 1 Tbsp. of the butter or margarine in a skillet. Add onion and sauté over medium heat until golden brown. In a large bowl, combine sautéed onion, beef, pork, rice, salt, and pepper.

Trim main stems of cabbage leaves. Spread one leaf flat. Depending on leaf size, place 2–3 Tbsp. filling on cabbage leaf near base. Fold bottom of leaf over filling, and then fold sides toward center. Roll Tightly. Repeat with remaining filling and cabbage leaves.

Heat 1 Tbsp. of the butter or margarine in a large skillet. Place filled cabbage leaves, seam down, in the skillet. Cover and cook over medium heat until browned, 8–10 minutes, turning once with a spatula.

Arrange cabbage rolls, seam down, in a medium roasting pan. Add 3 cups beef broth or bouillon. In a small bowl combine ½ cup broth or bouillon and tomato paste. Pour over stuffed cabbage. Cover and bake 40 minutes or until tender.

In a small skillet, melt remaining 2 Tbsp. butter or margarine. Stir flour into butter or margarine until smooth. Cook over medium heat, stirring until golden brown. Ladle 1 cup of the broth or bouillon from the stuffed cabbage into flour mixture; stir until blended. Pour mixture over stuffed cabbage. Cook uncovered until liquid bubbles and thickens slightly.

Place stuffed cabbage on a large platter. Pour juices into a serving bowl. Serve hot stuffed cabbage with pan juices.

Rice + meat + vegetable = one great meal!

I used this recipe one time and promised myself I would never cook it again. I don't know if it was the memories, the guilt of having enjoyed it for so many years, or the fact that I found the recipe cumbersome, but I could never bring myself to do it again. However, his (God's) Devine Will must have wanted me to share something with you, since He allowed a similar recipe to be sent to my email.

If your kitchen toys include a Crock-Pot or other slow cooker, you will enjoy the next recipe. I promise you it is easier and just as tasty.

Fancy Cabbage Rolls

1 lb. ground beef, browned
¼ c. cooked rice
1 egg
1 onion, minced
1 carrot, minced
1 tsp. salt
½ tsp. pepper
¼ c. cider vinegar
½ c. brown sugar
8 oz. canned tomato sauce
1 green cabbage

Mix ground beef, rice, egg, onion, carrot, salt, and pepper. In a separate bowl, mix together vinegar, brown sugar, and tomato sauce.

Drop cabbage in boiling water for 5–10 minutes. Remove 10 large leaves. Chop remaining cabbage and place in bottom of slow cooker. Place 2–4 Tbsp. of meat mixture in center of each whole leaf. Roll up and use toothpick to hold. Place each roll seam-down in slow cooker. Pour tomato-sauce mixture over rolls. Cover and cook on Low for 8–10 hours.

This is the perfect meal for a rainy day!

HELPFUL TIPS

Free advice from me to you:

- Try olive oil instead of margarine or shortening for frying and sautéing. Butter tastes good but olive oil is healthier.
- Instead of table salt, use sea salt or kosher salt; they are healthier.
- Aluminum foil should not touch your food, but it makes a great lid and covering.
- Fresh vegetables are best, followed by frozen.
- Cook with the wines that you drink.
- Rice milk, soy milk, and almond milk are good milk substitutes for the lactose intolerant.
- All recipes appear here as printed on the cards in the recipe box. My suggestions and changes are added with an asterisk (*).
- This book and most of the recipes within are not for the vegetarian or anyone with dietary restrictions.

GLOSSARY

c.: cup
lb.: pound
oz.: ounce
pkg.: package
Tbsp.: tablespoon
tsp.: teaspoon

blanch: To plunge food briefly into boiling water, then into cool water to stop the cooking process. This is done to firm the flesh, to loosen the skin (tomatoes) and to heighten and set the color, flavor, and nutrients prior to freezing.

carcinogen: a cancer-causing substance.

cream: To work one or more foods with a spoon, spatula, or hand mixer until smooth and creamy, rubbing the food against the sides of the bowl until the mixture is the consistency of cream.

cruciferous: belonging to a family of plants including the cabbage, turnip, and mustard.

detoxify: To remove harmful substances, toxins, or emotions from the body.

free radicals: an atom or group of atoms, either produced in the body by a natural biological process or introduced into the body by an outside source (such as tobacco smoke, toxins), that can damage cells.

fry pot: A pot that is used only to fry food in; it is deep enough to allow one to boil food in oil or deep-fry.

mince: to cut or chop food into very small pieces (smaller than chopped).

sauté: To cook quickly in a little oil, butter, or margarine.

RAINY-DAY SUNSHINE: SLOW-COOKED MEALS AND GRIEF-HEALING ASSIGNMENTS

Lillian was born in 1921. She was a child during the Great Depression, and she never forgot the soup lines; the WPA; the coal mines that did not hire colored men; having to shovel coal into her basement; or "Santa Claus" bringing her a Christmas gift of one apple, one orange, and three nuts.

During the Great Depression, everyone was poor and everyone was hungry; the coloreds, the Poles (Polish), and the Italians were all hungry. "The good thing about the Depression," according to Lillian, "was all men were equal. Hunger, unlike people, did not discriminate."

Two things my mother took with her through life were the importance of a good stew or soup and the gift of sharing food.

A rainy day is time set aside to work things out, to deal with grief and other emotions that are potential burdens to the spirit and soul. It is time set aside to honor your deity, pray, meditate. One need not be grieving or dealing with any issues to have a rainy day; it can simply be time set aside to hear and listen to the quiet voice of your angel, the Holy Spirit, and/or divine love. I refer to these days as my Sabbath. A friend of mine calls them "sanity day"— a day to regain your sanity.

Striving toward happiness in spite of the circumstances is the sunshine of a rainy day. Sometimes it is mandatory to take a day off from the world to reflect, pray, meditate, or just rejuvenate the soul. Since most of the time we prefer to attend to the various duties assigned to us, we take time for ourselves reluctantly, thinking that the desire to retreat must be caused by sad or blue feelings.

Depending on what one is dealing with spiritually and emotionally, a rainy day can be a day of hard work. I call this type of work "soul work" because it is work that lightens the burden on the soul. Rainy days are important and should occasionally be observed by everyone who has a soul. Do not forget to feed your body on your rainy day or while you do your soul work. A good meal can be in the making while you are working things out.

> *Be transformed by the renewing of your mind.*
> —Romans 12:2 (NIV)

Soul Work Assignment #1

Try writing your feelings or thoughts in a journal. Putting your thoughts and feelings on paper may help you deal with powerful emotions that you may need to express or release. Reading your journal entry out loud can be done the same day of journaling or during another rainy day. Journal writing and journal reading can be a cleansing, purging activity. It allows one to vent, rant, or do whatever to release some stuff, all emotional baggage that may be weighting on you. When done correctly and with honesty, journal reading and writing can be spiritually rewarding and far more beneficial than talking with a friend. Journaling for the purpose of cleansing and releasing should be done in a sacred manner: the entire activity is personal, the physical entries are private, and your expressions— what you feel, think, or say in your journal—are yours. Your journal should be shared with no one, and no one has the right or authority to discuss, agree or disagree with you on what you expressed. If you are in therapy, your therapist should have his or her own work for you; this assignment is to help you achieve serenity and inner peace.

Soul Work Assignment #2

If you don't find journal writing and reading very helpful, try this instead: write directly to whomever you have an issue with but cannot talk to. If you have an issue with someone who has died or is not physically present in your life, address that person. If your issue is a situation or an incident, not a person, address the situation or incident. You can either write in your journal, expressing what is bothering you, or write a letter directly addressed to the person, situation, or incident. Personally, I found writing directly to the problem gratifying.

When you begin the letter-writing task, make your letter short and to the point. You will write only one letter to one person or issue on one rainy day. Do not ramble on and on; do not repeat yourself. Name whomever you are talking to in the greeting, and state what the issues are, how the issue has bothered you, and how you feel. Sign your name or the name by which the person knew you. And then forgive. If you must forgive the person or situation, then forgive them. If you need to forgive yourself, then forgive yourself.

Allow your journal entry to simmer and then cool down—it may be in the best interests of your emotions or your spirit to take some time between the writing and the reading. After you've composed your letter and have calmed down, read the letter or journal entry aloud to a picture of the person, a doll, a chair—anything to represent the issue or the person.

If you feel you must read your letter to a living person, out of courtesy you should prepare the recipient for a serious encounter. It would be completely inappropriate to just walk up to a person and begin reading a letter describing your conflict with that person and your feelings about it, and then ending with a blurted, "But I forgive you!" Instead, tell the person that you have a conflict you've been struggling with and it is your desire to remove that burden. Ask, "Do I have your permission to proceed? It involves you." Once you have the recipient's permission, then begin in a place that provides privacy to both of you. If you do not get permission to continue, then you can complete this exercise by reading out loud to something that represents the person, such as a picture. Either way, remember to *forgive the person*, destroy the letter, and *release it to God*.

On one rainy day I talked to my mother (addressing her picture) and on another rainy day I talked to my health issue (addressing the test results). No, my mother did not return from the dead, but I released the guilt I carried. I let it go. While I continue to wrestle with a specific health issue, I was able to release my growing anger about the physical challenges associated with the disorder.

> *Get rid of all bitterness, rage and anger, brawling and slander, along with every form of malice.*
> —*Ephesians 4:31 (NIV)*

Soul Work Assignment #3

Last, but not the least effective, write in your journal to your deity and later read back to your deity what you wrote. Write as if you are talking to your god. This is the time to be frank and candid. Tell your god how you feel and what is bothering you. If you are angry, let your god know. If you are heartbroken, confused, tired of a situation, tell your god. Do you have questions and no answers? Ask your god why, if that is on your heart. You may or may not receive an answer, but you can always ask. I don't know about you and your god, but my god can handle my raw honesty and questions.

I found the time I spent writing to God extremely beneficial and most rewarding; it enabled me to tell God all that was troubling me. After I read this particular journal entry aloud, I felt relief and immeasurable peace.

> *In peace I will lie down and sleep, for you alone, Lord, make*
> *me dwell in safety.*
> *Psalm 4:8 (NIV)*

Soul Work Assignment #4

If you do not find it helpful to journal, write a letter, or converse with your god, then read God's word. I recommend Psalm 119—all 176 verses. Take your time with each section. You may need more than one rainy day to get through this assignment.

I recommend completing at least two assignments; it doesn't matter in what order they're completed. A rainy day is not a day of leisure or free time; it is a day of soul work, reflection, honest conversation with self, and a reckoning with the raw, frank dialogue. A rainy day is a time to be authentic with self and God. It can get ugly. Your sunshine will come more quickly and be brighter if you include God in your conversation and assignments. I also recommend completing only one assignment per day. Depending on how much stuff is involved, it may be better to complete an assignment on one day and read the entry aloud on another day.

All this work will make one hungry! That's why it is so important to begin preparing your rainy-day meal before you begin journaling and conversing authentically with yourself. At the end of the day you can enjoy a good meal.

> *O taste and see that the Lord is good; blessed is the one who takes refuge in him.*
> *—Psalm 34:8(NIV)*

Let's eat.

Barley Soup

This is perfect for a cold or rainy day or a day when one feels blue. Put on some good music; cook the barley and add the vegetables while you clean house, read, or whatever. The house will have that good-food smell while this is cooking.

½ c. scotch or pearl barley, uncooked

6 c. water*

1 c. diced carrots

½ c. diced green pepper

1/3 c. tomato puree

½ c. diced tomatoes, skin removed

½ c. diced celery

1 c. diced green beans

¾ tsp. salt

½–1 Tbsp. oregano

½–1 tsp. thyme

**For a more robust flavor, try a vegetable or chicken broth
in place of water and omit the salt.*

Simmer barley in water until tender, about 1–2 hours. Add remaining ingredients and simmer until vegetables are tender. If the barley or carrots soak up all the water, add a cup of chicken broth and continue. This provides enough for 3 people to enjoy a second helping.

Boston Baked Beans

This is a perfect item to cook while you are asleep or at work. Serve with ribs or a baked chicken and a salad. This is suitable for the slow cooker on Low for about 10 hours.

1 lb. navy beans (also called pea beans or small white beans)
½ lb. salt pork
1 medium onion, diced into ½" pieces
4 cloves garlic, finely chopped
1 c. tomato puree
1 tsp. salt
2 tsp. freshly ground black pepper
¼ c. dry mustard
1/3 c. maple sugar
1/3 c. molasses
2 bay leaves
3 Tbsp. cider vinegar

Cover the beans with warm water and soak for about 8 hours. Discard off-color and broken beans. Rinse and drain beans. Remove and discard the rind from half of the salt pork. Cut this part of salt pork into ½" pieces. Cut the remaining salt pork into ¾"–1" strips. Set aside.

Line the bottom of a heavy Dutch oven or slow cooker with the ½" pieces of salt pork. Place beans on top. In a separate pot, bring a quart of water to boil. Add garlic, tomato puree, salt, pepper, dry mustard, maple sugar, molasses, bay leaves, onion and vinegar to the water. Simmer for 1 minute. Mix well and pour over beans.

Preheat oven to 280°F. Cut strips of salt pork crosswise, about every inch, without slicing all the way through. This prevents the strips from curling while cooking. Place strips on top of beans and liquid. Cover pot and bake for 6 hours, checking to make sure liquid is barely covering beans. Add more hot water as needed. After 6 hours, uncover the pot and cook 1 additional hour. Remove strips of salt pork and stir thoroughly before serving.

FISH: FOOD FOR THE BRAIN

My mom did not have a problem with eating leftovers for breakfast. After all, food is food, any time of the day or night. She would eat cold chicken and potato salad in the morning while watching the Oprah show, and scrambled eggs and liver in the evening. That's how she was; she ate what she wanted when she wanted.

One year, while vacationing in Myrtle Beach, I became acquainted with fish, grits, scrambled egg, and biscuits for breakfast. As strange as that sounded to me, I ordered it because the price was so reasonable. It has been my favorite breakfast ever since.

Fish is the brain food and the stuff that Jesus ate. Like me and my mom, he prepared it for the first meal of the day.

> *Early in the morning, Jesus stood on the shore, but the disciples did not realize that it was Jesus. He called out to them, "Friends, haven't you any fish?"*
>
> *"No," they answered.*
>
> *He said, "Throw your net on the right side of the boat and you will find some." When they did, they were unable to haul the net in because of the large number of fish.*
>
> *Then the disciple whom Jesus loved said to Peter, "It is the Lord!" As soon as Simon Peter heard him say, "It is the Lord," he wrapped his outer garment around him (for he had taken it off) and jumped into the water. The other disciples followed in the boat, towing the net full of fish, for they were not far from the shore, about a hundred yards. When they landed, they saw a fire of burning coals there with fish on it, and some bread.*

Jesus said to them, "Bring some of the fish you have just caught." So Simon Peter climbed back into the boat and dragged the net ashore. It was full of large fish, 153, but even with so many the net was not torn. Jesus said to them, "Come and have breakfast."
—John 21:4–12 (NIV)

Salmon Burgers

2 6-oz. cans skinless, boneless salmon, drained
½ c. dry bread crumbs
4 green onions, finely chopped
¼ c. mayonnaise
2 eggs, beaten
1 Tbsp. parsley, minced
1 Tbsp. fresh-squeezed lemon juice
1¼ tsp. seafood seasoning, such as Old Bay
1 c. oil for frying
6 hamburger buns
mayonnaise or mustard for buns

Separate (flake) salmon with a fork in a medium bowl. Add bread crumbs, onions, mayonnaise, eggs, lemon juice, parsley, and seafood seasoning; mix well. Shape into 6 burgers. Grill or panfry until browned, about 3 minutes on each side. Serve on hamburger buns with mayonnaise and/or mustard.

Fish is the food for the human brain and heart. It is full of omega-3 fatty acids, an essential item the body needs but does not make. Salmon is a good source of omega-3.

Salmon Cakes

1 lb. salmon, either canned or fresh
1 small onion, chopped
1 large egg, beaten
1 c. sharp cheddar cheese, shredded
½ c. soft bread crumbs
¼ c. (or more) all-purpose flour
1 Tbsp. Worcestershire sauce
1 Tbsp. parsley, finely chopped
¼–½ tsp. hot pepper sauce (or to taste)
¼ tsp. freshly ground black pepper
¼ c. (½ stick) butter or margarine
lemon wedges

> My mom said anyone who did not eat fish probably did not have a good mind.

If using canned salmon, drain and remove cartilage and bones. Flake salmon. If using fresh salmon, place salmon in a pan, cover with hot water, and cook, covered, over medium-high heat for about 5 minutes. Turn over and cook for 5 more minutes. Remove from pan and flake salmon.

Combine salmon, onion, egg, cheese, bread crumbs, flour, Worcestershire sauce, parsley, hot sauce, and black pepper in medium bowl; mix well.

Shape salmon mixture into rounds about ½" thick, using about 1/3 c. of the mixture for each cake. Sprinkle additional flour on plate or board. Dredge patties in flour, coating well but dusting off excess. Chill patties in refrigerator at least 30 minutes.

Melt butter or margarine in a large skillet over medium-high heat until foamy and hot. Add patties and brown on both sides until cooked through, about 5 minutes per side. Drain on paper towels.

Serve midday with lemon wedges or serve with breakfast: eggs, grits, and toast.

Baked Salmon Loaf

I always referred to this as fish loaf. Now that I am older and have been instructed in the benefits of salmon in our diets, I have a new appreciation for this quick, nutritious dish. It is the best leftover food in the world, and it makes a great sandwich, warm or cold.

- 1 c. celery
- 1 c. onion, minced fine
- ½ lb. fresh mushrooms, chopped
- 2 lemons
- 2 1-lb. cans salmon, undrained
- ½ c. skim milk
- 2 eggs, beaten, or 4 egg whites
- 3 Tbsp. fresh parsley or dill weed, chopped
- 2 c. bread crumbs

Combine celery, onion, and mushrooms. Add juice from lemons. Grate the lemon peel and add to mixture. Add remaining ingredients (including liquid from canned salmon) and mix well.

Spray a 9" nonstick loaf pan with cooking spray and pack mixture inside. Bake at 375°F for 40–50 minutes. Cut into slices and serve hot. Makes 8 servings.

Leftovers can be frozen and eaten at another time.

Red Snapper Soup

Fish soup is a warm, liquid food for the brain! It is light but can be filling when served with wild rice. Red Snapper Soup is prepared in 40 minutes and has a short cook time. The recipe is presented in two parts: the soup and the fish.

Soup Base

2 Tbsp. olive oil

2 carrots, chopped

2 celery ribs, chopped

2 garlic cloves, chopped

1 onion, chopped

½ red bell pepper

½ green bell pepper

12 crushed whole white peppercorns

1 bay leaf

3 Tbsp. tomato paste

2 tsp. fresh thyme, chopped

2 tsp. fresh rosemary, chopped

2 tsp. fresh cilantro, chopped

8 c. vegetable broth

3 Tbsp. unsalted butter

2 Tbsp. all-purpose flour

1 Tbsp. cornstarch

salt to taste

Fish

2 small onions, finely chopped

3 ribs celery, finely chopped

1 or 2 filets red snapper, 10 oz. total

¼ c. sherry*

I use red wine.

Soup Base

Heat oil in a Dutch oven over medium heat. Add carrots, celery, garlic, onion, and bell peppers; cook, stirring frequently, about 4 minutes. Stir in peppercorns, bay leaf, tomato paste, thyme, rosemary, and cilantro. Cook 2 minutes. Add 7 cups of the broth; heat to a boil.

Melt butter in a small pan; add flour and cornstarch. Stir constantly while cooking, 4–5 minutes. *Slowly* stir in the remaining cup of broth. Use a wire whisk and/or the back of a wooden spoon until mixture (a roux) is smooth. Add this roux to the soup base; cover and simmer over medium heat for 20 minutes. Strain the mixture through a strainer or cheesecloth to remove all solids, and return the clear broth to the pot. Add salt to taste, if necessary.

Red Snapper

Add onions and celery to a pot of boiling water; cook until soft (about 3 minutes). Remove vegetables with a slotted spoon and add to the soup broth. Boil fish in the same water until cooked through. Remove fish from the water and flake with a fork. Stir the fish and sherry/wine into the soup base, heat thoroughly, and serve.

The following chowder is easy and fast to put together. It is even better the second day. I recommend cooking this the day before your rainy day, refrigerating, and reheating for lunch.

Bourbon Street Chowder

  1 lb. fresh medium shrimp, shelled and deveined*
  3 Tbsp. butter or margarine
  1 c. chopped onion
  1 large clove garlic, minced
  1 large bay leaf
  2 10.5-oz. cans condensed chicken with rice soup
  2 10.75-oz. cans condensed cream of potato soup
  2 soup cans of water
  1 16-oz. can tomatoes, chopped
  2 c. cooked chicken or turkey, cubed (leftovers okay)
  1 10-oz. pkg. frozen cut okra
  2 Tbsp. hot sauce
  1 Tbsp. Worcestershire sauce
  In the margins, Momma added:
  1 Tbsp. brown sugar
  2 Tbsp. lemon juice
  crabmeat

*or a 1 lb. bag of frozen raw shrimp cleaned and deveined.

In a large pot cook shrimp in butter or margarine with the onion, garlic and bay leaf until tender. Stir in soups. Gradually blend in water. Add remaining ingredients. Bring to a boil and reduce heat. Simmer 10 minutes or until okra is soft. Stir occasionally. Remove bay leaf before serving. Makes 14 cups.

The following recipe is from section seven, page thirty-four, of the New Orleans *Times-Picayune*, Sunday, April 14, 1974. The Barbecued Shrimp and Shrimp Ball recipes, elsewhere in this book, are from the same page. I've cooked this Stuffed Red Snapper dish many times, especially for Christmas and other holiday meals. If you like fish, you will love this. Momma, how and where did you get a paper from New Orleans?

Stuffed Red Snapper

> 1 large red snapper-(6–8 lbs.)*
> Salt to taste
> 2 slices bacon**
> 1 lemon

Stuffing:

> 1 small onion, finely chopped
> 1 large clove garlic, minced or pressed
> ½ rib celery, finely chopped
> ½ medium bell pepper, finely chopped
> 1 Tbsp. parsley, finely chopped
> ½ stick butter or oleo (margarine)
> ½ c. seasoned bread crumbs
> 1½ c. crabmeat (fresh or canned)
> 1 tsp. salt
> ½ tsp. black pepper

> *Ask your butcher to scale and clean your fish.*
> **If you don't eat pork, omit the bacon and add garlic—and, if desired, a bit of cayenne pepper—to the crabmeat stuffing,*

for a strong, hot flavor. Sprinkle Lillian's Seasoning (see below) on the fish.

Wash and scale the fish, if not already done. Slice a pocket on one side; salt inside the pocket.

Sauté onion, garlic, celery, bell pepper, and parsley in butter or margarine. Add seasoned bread crumbs, crabmeat, salt, and pepper. Stuff this mixture inside the fish.

Lay a slice of bacon inside the fish, on top of the stuffing. Lay another slice of bacon on the outside of the fish. Cover and bake at 350°F for 50 minutes. Uncover and bake for an additional 10 minutes. Squeeze a lemon over the fish and serve.

Lillian's Special Seasoning

I buy a particular seasoning salt and often use it in place of regular white salt. However, I keep the following Special Seasoning mix in an emptied seasoning container for my baked meats and fish. As you use and empty a bottle of seasoning salt, pepper, or any spice, wash off the label, type "[Your name]'s Special Seasoning" on a printable address label, and place the label on the container. With the small holes and large opening from the original packaging, you will feel extremely professional and adept every time you use your Special Seasoning.

Next, prepare the sauce.

Barbecue Sauce

1½ c. catsup
¾ c. chili sauce
½ c. vinegar
6 Tbsp. Worcestershire sauce
6 Tbsp. brown sugar, firmly packed
3 Tbsp. fresh lemon juice
1 Tbsp. paprika
2¼ tsp. salt
1 clove garlic, crushed
¼ tsp. hot pepper sauce
¼ tsp. black pepper
onion and lemon, sliced thinly

Combine ketchup, chili sauce, vinegar, Worcestershire sauce, brown sugar, lemon juice, paprika, salt, garlic, and hot sauce with 1½ c. water in a large saucepan. Heat to the boiling point. Reduce heat and simmer 30–45 minutes until sauce thickens and is a good consistency for basting.

The Best Oven-Roasted Ribs

3 slabs of pork spareribs (9 lbs.) or 4 slabs of baby back ribs (8 lbs.)

Marinate meat; apply dry rub.

Adjust oven rack to upper middle position and preheat oven to 250°F. To prepare your Dry Rub, mix sugar, paprika, pepper, garlic powder, and salt in a small bowl. Brush both sides of each slab with mustard, and then sprinkle the dry rub on both sides.

Roast ribs until fork-tender: 2–3 hours for spareribs and 1½–2 hours for baby back ribs.

If you want to apply sauce: pour off the fat, turn on the broiler, turn ribs meat-side down, and brush ribs with half the sauce. Put pan under the broiler until the sauce glazes and bubbles vigorously, about 3–5 minutes. Remove pan, turn ribs, brush with remaining sauce, and return to broiler for another 3-5 minutes. When the ribs are shiny and sticky remove from the oven and let stand 5–10 min before serving.

Or try this recipe for oven barbecued ribs

Barbecued Ribs

Place ribs in a shallow pan. Sprinkle with 1 tsp. salt and ½ tsp. pepper. Bake at 450°F for 30 minutes. Remove pan, drain fat, put ribs meat-side down and baste with sauce. Reduce oven temperature to 300°F and bake 30 minutes more. Turn ribs meat-side up; brush with sauce. Top ribs with an onion slice if desired. Bake about 1 hour more, brushing frequently with the sauce, until ribs are tender and browned. If desired, add lemon slices to ribs during last half hour of baking.

Barbecued Shrimp

4 lbs. large shrimp

4 sticks margarine

¾ tsp. crushed red pepper

2 tsp. garlic salt

2 tsp. dry barbecue seasoning

3 tsp. Worcestershire sauce

2 tsp. paprika

¾ tsp. salt

Clean, shell, and devein the shrimp; (Devein by removing the shrimp's black seam or streak each shrimp using the blade of a sharp knife) place in a shallow baking dish. (You can buy a bag of frozen deveined shrimp; be sure to remove the shells.)

Make sauce: melt the margarine in a saucepan and add remaining ingredients. Add sauce to the shrimp. Bake at 300°F for 40 minutes, basting often.

Serve hot with warm French bread to dip in the sauce. Serves 4.

Another Barbecue Sauce

1 stick butter, melted

½ c. vinegar

1 c. water

½ c. catsup

1 large onion, grated

2 cloves garlic, crushed

½ c. brown sugar

2 bay leaves

1 Tbsp. dry mustard

1 tsp. chili powder

2 Tbsp. steak sauce

1 tsp. salt

1 tsp. black pepper

¼ tsp. cayenne pepper

Combine all ingredients. Simmer slowly for about 20 minutes, stirring frequently.

Remove bay leaves and use sauce immediately or refrigerate for future use.

THE SALAD BAR

Did you know that grieving, depression, and a general feeling of malaise all consume energy? Some grievers tend to lose their appetite for food or their ability to taste. Others develop an insatiable appetite for comfort foods and all the stuff that tastes good but is not healthy, because those comfort foods can trigger happy thoughts or a general feeling of well-being. In other words, grief causes some people to stop eating and encourages others to overeat rich, unhealthy foods.

A large vegetable salad is the nutritional solution for the grieving person, the stressed, the busy, the depressed person, the heartbroken and the sad. Salads are easy to make and, when done right, are packed with powerful vitamins and minerals that provide antioxidants and energy. A good salad will also boost and protect the immune system.

The best salad is built on the foundation of greens: dark leafy greens such as raw spinach, kale, spring greens or baby greens, cabbage, green-leaf lettuce, or romaine lettuce. Avoid iceberg lettuce because it has almost no nutritional value. Build on a solid salad foundation by adding fresh, raw, unprocessed vegetables in a wide array of colors. Not only will this be appealing to the eye, it will also be packed with everything the body needs to build and replenish. The more colors in your salad the prettier and more appetizing it will appear. In addition, the different colorful vegetables will provide more availability of nutrients and minerals to your body's cells.

You will be off to a great start toward healing with a bowl of edible vitamins and minerals. The greens listed above will provide you with iron and vitamins A, E, and K. Spinach, a source of iron, will build healthy blood cells. Vitamin A supports eye and respiratory health and maintains a healthy immune system. It also promotes strong bones, healthy skin and hair, and strong teeth. Vitamin E slows the aging process, maintains positive cholesterol ratios, protects the lungs from pollution, provides endurance-boosting oxygen, and alleviates fatigue. Vitamin K keeps the blood vessels strong, promotes blood clotting, and prevents abnormal bleeding.

In addition to vitamins, greens also contain protein and the minerals folate, manganese, chromium, and potassium.

- Folate produces healthy red blood cells, reduces the risk of stroke, protects the heart, promotes healthy skin, and helps maintain hair color. It has been said to be a natural antidepressant.
- Manganese keeps fatigue away, boosts memory, and helps prevent osteoporosis (a weakening of the bones).
- Chromium helps normalize blood pressure and insulin levels. It prevents sugar cravings and drops in energy.
- Potassium regulates the body's water balance and normalizes heart rhythms. It sends oxygen to the brain and aids clear thinking.

As you can see, the greens alone, without other vegetables, are an invaluable source of really good stuff. Without a good salad, one may end up tired and forgetful, with bad skin, prematurely gray hair, soft bones, high blood pressure, and high sugar levels that could lead to prediabetes. Your teeth could go and your heartbeat could be irregular. As Momma always said, "Eat your vegetables!"

Now let's put some color on those greens. My favorite color is red, therefore my salad must have tomatoes, chili peppers, red onions, red bell peppers, maybe radishes, and definitely beets. Tomatoes contain high levels of carotenoid lycopene, a substance known for fighting prostate cancer, and acids (chlorogenic and coumaric) that keep lungs healthy by blocking the effects of carcinogens. Meat eaters and smokers really should include tomatoes in their diet and cook tomatoes with their meats; the chlorogenic acids in tomatoes block the toxin nitrosamine in cigarettes and also block the sodium nitrates used as a preservative in meats. Beets have been used for centuries to detoxify and build the blood. My mother made a point to cook and pickle beets for her salads because she knew beets were good for the anemic. Beets are high in folic acid, iron, and calcium, and contain betaine, a compound that detoxifies the liver.

It looks like beets and tomatoes are the most valuable of the red vegetables—but the others will make the salad pretty. The chili peppers will make it spicy, the radishes will provide a good crunch, and the onions … oh, how I love onions of all colors!

A word to the wise: include cruciferous vegetables in your diet and add them to your salad. Cruciferous vegetables include cabbage (all colors), cauliflower, brussels sprouts, broccoli, kale, bok choy, radishes, and watercress. This family of vegetables takes its name from the Latin word *cruciferae* ("cross bearing") and from the shape of its flowers, whose four petals resemble a cross. Cruciferous vegetables are full of fiber and more vitamins and minerals that are known for lowering the risks of cancer. They are renowned for their ability to cleanse by producing a smooth elimination. A salad with sliced or shredded cabbage, raw broccoli and/or cauliflower, and sliced radishes will guarantee a healthy elimination. Most importantly, of all the vegetables, the cruciferous vegetables' properties are the most potent when raw or slightly steamed.

Is it not ironic that a vegetable that bears a cross is the most potent food to fight cancer and stress? The cross-bearing vegetables also provide protection to the digestive system and the immune system. O the power of the cross!

The salad bowl should also include the color yellow: carrots, yellow peppers, sweet potatoes, and yellow summer squash. Raw sweet potatoes can be diced or sliced and added to the salad; they will resemble the carrot in look but not in taste. The yellow vegetables are all rich in beta-carotene, a powerful free-radical scavenger that prevents damage to cells. Free radicals are responsible for clogged arteries and heart disease, cataracts, blood-vessel damage, inflammatory diseases, arthritis, asthma, and some cancers. You do not want free radicals living in your system. Has your mother or grandmother ever told you that carrots are good for your eyes?

Make your salad fit for royalty (you!) by including the color purple. Purple vegetables include purple cabbage, purple endive, and eggplant. Vegetarians are familiar with the properties of the eggplant. It is used as a meat substitute in dishes like lasagna and is a protein source. Cabbage of any color is a natural cleanser, moving out harmful compounds from the body and eliminating toxins, carcinogens, and free radicals. In other words, cabbage is a natural detoxifier. And remember, cabbage is a cruciferous vegetable.

All peppers (green, yellow, orange, and red) and carrots contain vitamin C. Vitamin C is involved in the formation of collagen, a substance needed in the growth and repair of tissue cells, gums, blood vessels, bones, and teeth.

Your white vegetables would include onion, cauliflower, (a cruciferous vegetable), garlic and mushrooms. You may want to include them to add color, texture and flavor to your salad.

Green vegetables are broccoli, cucumbers, bell peppers, zucchini, asparagus, and okra. Broccoli contains protein (twenty-six percent of its content is protein) and provides super antioxidants. Broccoli is a cruciferous vegetable, which means you can depend on its cleansing properties. Green bell peppers contain vitamin C, an immune booster.

The rainbow colors inside the salad bowl would encourage most people to eat the contents, even grief stricken persons. Fruit may be included in the salad for additional color. Any berry: black or blue, strawberries or raspberries, may be added. Apple slices with their peeling gives a sweet/tart taste and contributes a healthy crunch. The idea is to present a dish that is visually appealing and nutritious.

The act of crying can literally drain a body of energy and nutrients. Sometimes grieving or stressed people don't feel like eating, or lose interest in it. Those who live alone may simply forget to eat, especially if their situation requires a major change, such as continuing life without their beloved. It takes time to adjust to the new situation of eating or living alone. The point is: anyone can quickly and easily regain the nutrients lost during the grieving process—by eating well. During a period of mourning, how often one eats is not as important as *what* one eats. A forkful or two of salad or a few raw vegetables and dip may be more beneficial than "a good breakfast."

Below are two different coleslaw recipes to try. I prefer the Cape Cod. Serve either with a soup or baked fish. Today you can skip shredding cabbage and buy a bag of coleslaw mix, but buying a fresh cabbage is cheaper and healthier. It won't hurt a thing if you add shredded carrots to either recipe.

Cape Cod Coleslaw

> 6 c. shredded cabbage (about 2 lbs.)
> 2 Tbsp. cider vinegar
> 2 Tbsp. vegetable or olive oil
> 1/3 c. sour cream
> 1/3 c. mayonnaise
> ¾ tsp. salt
> ¼ tsp. pepper

Mix cabbage with vinegar and oil. Blend in sour cream, mayonnaise, and salt pepper. Chill thoroughly before serving.

Coleslaw

> *(Adapted from a recipe from Shaw's Crab House)*

> 2/3 c. sugar
> ½ tsp. white pepper
> ½ tsp. salt
> ¼ c. white vinegar
> 1 c. mayonnaise
> 1 c. sour cream
> 1 green cabbage, shredded

In a large bowl, dissolve sugar, pepper, and salt in vinegar. Mix in mayonnaise and sour cream. Add cabbage to dressing. Toss to mix. Adjust seasoning to taste. Chill and serve.

Cucumber Sour Cream Dressing

1½ Tbsp. cider vinegar

2 tsp. sugar

½ tsp. salt

1 c. sour cream or yogurt

1½ cup cucumber, peeled and chopped

In a bowl, blend vinegar, sugar, and salt. Fold in sour cream or yogurt and cucumber. Serve dressing over sliced beets, onions, and tomatoes.

There were always salads in my mother's refrigerator. *Always!* And potato salad was a staple. Here are her best and favorite salads from the salad section. Momma's potato salad, served on lettuce with fancy little crackers, would take your mind off of your bills, a death, an illness—anything. Potato salad, a cup of coffee, perhaps a slice of cake … mmmmm.

My Momma's Potato Salad

  5 lbs. white potatoes (about 20 potatoes)

  3 c. mayonnaise

  2 Tbsp. vinegar

  2 tsp. Seasoned Salt

  ¾ tsp. pepper

  3 tsp. sugar

  1 c. celery, thinly sliced

  1 c. onions, chopped

  6 hard-boiled eggs, chopped

  1/3 c. green peppers, chopped

  pimientos, about 2 Tbsp. (optional)

Boil the potatoes until done. Drain and let cool. Peel and cut into small cubes.

In a large bowl, stir together mayonnaise, vinegar, seasoned salt, and pepper until smooth. Add remaining ingredients; toss to coat well. Cover and chill.

Easy Chicken Salad

3–4 whole chicken breasts, cooked, boned and cut into ½"
cubes

1 tsp. lemon pepper

6 stalks celery, chopped

1–2 tsp. capers (optional)

1–2 Tbsp. almond pieces (optional)*

4 sliced scallions

1/3 c. sour cream**

½ c. mayonnaise

1 tsp. dried dill

1–2 tsp. salt (to taste)

1 c. grape halves

Chopped walnuts or pecans will also do.
** *If dairy does not agree with you, replace with Miracle*
Whip or extra mayonnaise.

Toss together the chicken cubes, lemon pepper, celery, capers (if using), nuts (if using), and scallions. For dressing, combine sour cream, mayonnaise, dill, and salt. Mix dressing with chicken salad. Fold in grapes. Serves 4–6.

We referred to these next two salads as summer salads. They are both filling and cooling. I choose to serve the Three-Bean Salad with spring greens; Momma served hers on a bed of lettuce.

Three-Bean Salad

  1 c. soy or wax beans, shelled

  1 c. (can) kidney beans, drained

  1 c. (can) cut green beans, drained

  2/3 c. sweet Spanish onion, thinly sliced

  ½ cup celery, thinly sliced

  2 cloves garlic

  ½ c. white vinegar

  ¼ c. oil

  ¼ c. sugar

  ¼ tsp. oregano

  1 tsp. salt

  ¼ tsp. pepper

Cover soybeans or wax beans in water and boil for 8–10 minutes. Drain and mix with kidney beans, green beans, onion, celery, and garlic in a large bowl.

In a saucepan, mix vinegar, oil, and sugar; heat until sugar dissolves. Cool slightly. Stir oregano, salt, and pepper into vinegar mixture. Pour over vegetables and toss lightly. Chill overnight. Remove garlic and serve.

Seven-Cup Salad, Fruit Salad, or Punch-Bowl Salad

1 c. canned crushed pineapple, drained

1 c. seedless green grapes

1 c. miniature marshmallows

1 c. coconut

1 c. mandarin oranges, drained

1 c. sour cream*

1 c. bananas, sliced

or flavored yogurt

Momma's note: "Use the whole can for all ingredients and rename this 'Seven-Can Salad.'"

Combine all ingredients. Refrigerate overnight before serving. For beauty, cover the surface with Cool Whip or layer it: salad, Cool Whip, salad, etc., ending with Cool Whip on top.

This salad has made an appearance at many office parties, showers, potlucks, and family dinners. We like to serve it in a clear glass punch bowl, placed in the center of the table for a dramatic effect.

COMFORT MY PEOPLE

Comfort, comfort my people, says your God. Speak tenderly ...
—Isaiah 40:1 (NIV)

Oh, the comfort and inner warmth some foods bring. Heavy meats; thick gravies; gooey sweets; cheesy, messy, dripping, and greasy stuff tastes *so* good! It may not be good for you, but it definitely is good to you. That rich, buttery flavor ... the full and satisfied feeling after we eat ... and then we fall asleep.

Comfort is what you seek while healing, while "getting over it," while recuperating from grief. Wherever you initially find solace, consolation, relief, or an escape from the overbearing feelings that disappointment leaves behind—that may be where you will stay until you feel like moving on.

You might stay where you find relief until you feel ... like ... moving ... on.

Hopefully, prayerfully, one may merely withdraw or act strange for a short period. The grief-stricken person might wander into the zone of eating or overeating. That would not be too bad; eating is a safer alternative than drinking or using/abusing drugs. Seeking relief through food has its merits and downside in comparison to repeated acts of wild, impulsive sex with persons you hardly know. Don't laugh! Some emotions push people into places where they would never venture under normal circumstances.

Speaking about bad places, it is not unusual to do things out of character while running away from the pain of grief or disappointment. Many people have become romantically involved too soon after a breakup with or the death of the person they loved. What the body is prepared to do may not be equal to what the heart and spirit are ready for; your heart might not be ready to open and share with another person, even if your body is ready to get physical. Whether the loss is due to death, separation, divorce, or illness, having sex with one person while the heart, spirit, and perhaps the soul are with another person is not the path to recovery from grief.

It is natural to seek comfort in whatever makes you feel good. If lying next to someone and being held make you feel good, then of course that is what you will choose. If eating all the foods Momma cooked brings back good memories and you feel good every time you eat, then you will eat and eat and eat into a new size. If drinking helps you to forget or drugs deaden the pain you feel inside, then those may be what you choose to get through it. However, this chapter is not for helping you just get through—it is here to assist you to recovery and the return to your whole self.

The path to recovery is in confiding your anguish to your very own confidant. I recommend the Holy Spirit. The Holy Spirit is the helper or comforter Jesus sent to humankind to help Jesus in his absence. The Holy Spirit is *our* helper as well. The Holy Spirit is an extension of Jesus and a helper to us in times when we feel we can go no further. He gives us strength when we are weak, confidence when we are afraid, companionship when we are lonely, courage when we are fearful, guidance when we are confused or in need of direction, peace when we are angry or in turmoil. He soothes the brokenhearted and calms the worried, the anxious, and the troubled.

The Holy Spirit will meet you at your needs and supply all your needs. If you need conversation, the Holy Spirit will talk to you. If you need a touch or a hug, the Holy Spirit will envelop you so that you feel embraced. The Holy Spirit will release you from all unnecessary feelings of guilt. If you make an attempt to forgive someone—if you just *try* to forgive—the Holy Spirit will remove all animosity and horrible feelings you may have toward the person you are forgiving.

He (The Holy Spirit) will comfort you while you cry, and he acts as a telepathic mediator. You can be alone, crying, hungry, and feeling truly desolate, and the Holy Spirit will send someone to your house with a sandwich, a dish, or an invitation to dinner. The Holy Spirit will intercede and intervene at the right time to deliver you out of misery or unhappiness.

Freedom from grief and heartbreak can be yours through a belief in God. You can be released from the prison of (feeling) alone or lonely by accepting God and all of God's gifts. The overwhelming sensation of utter loneliness that may follow the loss of someone you dearly loved can be overcome by accepting and embracing the gifts God gave to each of us.

One gift God gave us is his son Jesus. Another gift God gave us is the Holy Spirit, and yet another gift from God is Peace. God also gave us a friend, and that "friend" is found in the acceptance of God's son, Jesus. Jesus walked the earth over two thousand years ago among regular people who were broken, oppressed, damaged or wounded. Jesus healed the sick and the broken. He restored vision to the blind. He picked up those who were down and weak and gave them strength. Jesus healed the minds, bodies and the spirit of anyone who needed healing.

He was concerned and had compassion for the impoverished. He fully understood the society he lived in and he also knew that sickness and death of one person affected the whole family. Widows and single women who had no man or no one to care for them were at risk of poverty and death, but Jesus resurrected their dead and returned them to the mothers and wives. He restored the minds of the mentally ill by releasing the evil spirits inside their bodies and commanding them to leave. Each time Jesus healed or restored or resurrected, he sent the newly restored person back to their family or back to their community.

You may not believe or understand how Jesus can help you but I assure you his helper, The Comforter or The Holy Spirit, *is* the greatest helper.

Yes, Jesus lives and continue to perform miracles through his helper, the Holy Spirit—the Comforter, the Friend, or Truth. Jesus' helper has many names, but the name I call him is *Holy Spirit*. Read these words spoken by Jesus to the men whom he was a friend to, whom he taught and spent a great deal of time with:

> *I will talk to the Father, and he will provide you another Friend so that you will always have someone with you. This Friend is the Spirit of Truth. The godless world can't take him in because it doesn't have eyes to see him, doesn't know what to look for. But you know him already because he has been staying with you, and will even be in you!*
> *—John 14:16–20 (The Message Bible)*

For those of you who are wondering how this "Friend" will help you or how it will operate, believe this:

The Friend, the Holy Spirit whom the Father will send at my request, will make everything plain to you. He will remind you of all the things I have told you. I'm leaving you well and whole. That's my parting gift to you. Peace. I don't leave you the way you are used to being left—feeling abandoned, bereft. So don't be upset. Don't be distraught.
—*John 14:26–27 (The Message Bible)*

The Old Testament is a collection of thirty-nine separate books that talk about a God and his chosen people, his favorites. These books are full of stories of God's love, the lives and battles of his favorite people, and their history, literature, songs, and poetry. The stories reveal how God communicated to his people—first through his chosen leader, Moses, and later through a series of prophets, people he chose to talk to and use as his mouthpiece.

One of the most fascinating characters in the Old Testament is David. David was a boy shepherd whom God selected to reign as king over God's people. David soon became the powerful King David, and as king he committed some horrible acts. But King David led the most courageous battles of war for his people. As a result, Saul, the former king, persecuted David in an effort to destroy him. David ran and hid for years from Saul and Saul's men (soldiers or paid assassins).

David was also a harp player, and while he was running and hiding, he wrote many songs and poems to God on the subjects of loneliness, feeling abandoned, and seeking God's presence and forgiveness. David's works are a general crying-out to the Lord.

David knew a little something about grief, emotional pain, and loneliness. He was acquainted with fear; he experienced the humiliation of being lied on and sought for an imaginary offense against the government. His life and lifestyle were turned upside down when he lived for years in exile, running from King Saul and his soldiers. David and his followers hid in a cave for months to escape murder at the hands of Saul's men. He was acquainted with disappointment: his children kept him in turmoil. His newborn son died, his daughter was raped by one of his sons, and his own son rebelled against him in an effort to overthrow King David and take over the throne and the monarchy. However, in spite of his experiences, King David never gave up on God; he never accepted that God had forgotten or left him. Today many of us continue to read the poems and songs written by King David; they are now known as Psalms.

I have found comfort in many of the Psalms and I share them with you so that you too may find comfort. Between David's writings and the words of Jesus, one should never feel lonely or abandoned. Regardless of how we feel or what we think, we are "alone" because we choose to be alone. King David knew that. Today we have the spirit of Jesus and the presence of the Holy Spirit to comfort us, and we also have Jesus' promise that he will never leave us:

> *And be sure of this—that I am with you always, even to the*
> *end of the world.*
> *—Matthew 28:20 (The Catholic Living Bible Paraphrased)*

If you are convinced that you are utterly alone, then invite Jesus, God, and the Holy Spirit into your life and into your heart and you will never be alone again. It takes only one invitation to receive a lifelong friend. He will stay as long as he is welcomed.

In Revelation, Jesus tells us:

Here I am! I stand at the door and knock. If anyone hears my voice and opens the door, I will come in and eat with that person, and they with me.
—Revelation 3:20 (NIV)

The door that Jesus knocks on is your heart. There is no doorknob, at least not on the outside. The only way he can enter is if you open the door from the inside and allow him in. Send him your invitation right now.

Most of us are not going to receive the miracle of having our deceased loved one return from the dead and resume life with us, although with God, anything is possible. When grief is present the goal is to become restored and return to our family and community. The reason why we must return to our family and community is we are needed to assist someone else that is living through their heartache. Jesus asked all those he healed to return to their community: The 10 lepers cleansed (Luke 17:14), the woman about to get stoned for adultery (John 8:1-11), Jairus' daughter (Luke 8:54), the man who lived in the cemetery (Luke 8:38-39) to go back, or return. All of the afflicted either removed their selves from society or were forced to leave due to the laws in placed (such as lepers).

That same Jesus wants you to return to your family and community when you heal. When you return, take someone something to eat!

As we go through my mother's recipes, make room for a new guest in your life, if you have not already received him.

53

> *Open your mouth and taste, open your eyes and see—how good God is. Blessed are you who run to him.*
> *—Psalm 34:8 (The Message Bible)*

This section offers food for comfort. Each recipe will yield enough for you to share with others and enjoy leftovers.

Smothered Turkey Wings

6 turkey wings
1 Tbsp. vegetable oil
1 Tbsp. salt
1 tsp. ground pepper
1 tsp. garlic powder
1 tsp. poultry seasoning
1 tsp. onion powder

Sauce:

1 c. butter
2 celery ribs, chopped
1 medium onion, chopped
1 tsp. dried thyme
1 tsp. pepper
7 Tbsp. all-purpose flour
6 c. turkey or chicken broth
2 c. milk

Brush wings with vegetable oil; place in large roasting pan. Stir together salt, pepper, garlic powder, poultry seasoning, and onion powder in a medium bowl; sprinkle mixture over turkey wings. Bake at 350°F until browned, 45–60 minutes.

For sauce, melt butter in a large Dutch oven. Add celery and onion; cook over medium low heat until soft but not brown, about 5 minutes. Remove the vegetables and set aside. Add the flour, a tablespoon at a time to your melted better, stirring the paste until it browns. Continue to add flour until it is gone. Smooth any lumps with the back of your spoon. Stir and watch the mixture slowly brown. Slowly add the broth to the browned flour. Again, smooth all lumps with the back of your spoon. When all the broth is added, use a wire whisk to rid the sauce of lumps. If there are any lumps of flour in the sauce remove them. This mixture is called a roux (pronounced Roo) and is the foundation of all sauces and soups. Add the vegetables, pepper and thyme to the sauce. Heat to a boil; reduce heat and simmer uncovered, 20 minutes. Strain sauce through a sieve and return to pan. Slowly whisk in milk; this will thicken the sauce. Stir constantly until sauce returns to a simmer. DO NOT BOIL. Pour sauce over turkey wings, cover pan, and cook in the oven at 350 degrees **until tender**, about 1 hour.

Chicken Supreme

(from Evelyn Tucker, a good friend of my mother, from Steubenville, Ohio)

1 stewing hen or large fryer, 14–15 lbs.
1 stalk celery, finely chopped
1 small onion, chopped
¼ c. butter
6–8 c. bread crumbs
sage to taste
the broth from the cooked chicken
1 can cream of chicken soup
1 small bag of potato chips

Cook chicken until tender by boiling in salted water. Remove meat from bones and place it in a buttered baking pan.

Dressing: Sauté celery and onion in butter and add it to the bread crumbs; add sage to taste. In a buttered baking pan, place one layer of chicken, then a layer of dressing, alternating. Mix the can of cream of chicken soup with a can of the broth from the cooked chicken. Pour this mixture over the layers of chicken and dressing.

Crumble the potato chips over the top to brown and form a topping. Bake at 350°F for 1½ hours.

Loretta Lynn's Chicken and Dumplings

Chicken

1 whole 5-lb. stewing chicken, cleaned
1 small onion, peeled and quartered
2 small stalks celery, diced
2–3 quarts boiling water
salt and pepper to taste

Dumplings

2 c. all-purpose four
½ tsp. salt
¼ tsp. baking powder
½ stick butter
3 eggs
1/3 c. milk

Put chicken in large stockpot. Add onion, celery, boiling water, salt, and pepper. Cover and let simmer slowly, 3–4 hours, until fork-tender.

Dumplings: Place dry ingredients in bowl. Cut butter into flour mixture. In a separate bowl, combine eggs with milk; stir into butter-flour mixture to make firm dough. Roll dough on floured board. Cut or break into small pieces. Drop a few pieces at a time into simmering chicken stock, cooking until done (about 2–3 minutes).

> *The Lord is close to the brokenhearted and saves those who are crushed in spirit.*
> *—Psalm 34:18 (NIV)*

Meat Loaf

This is my mother's "poor girl meat loaf." She would always remind me, "Be sure to use ground *chuck*, not ground beef." Momma's "better" recipe requires three meats.

2 eggs

¾ c. milk

½ c. seasoned dry bread crumbs

½ c. onion, chopped

1 garlic clove, chopped

2 Tbsp. parsley

salt to taste

¼ c. green pepper, chopped

½ tsp. sage

1½–2 lbs. ground chuck

½ tsp. ground black pepper

Topping

¼ c. ketchup

2 Tbsp. brown sugar

½ tsp. dry mustard

Combine eggs and milk. Stir in bread crumbs, onion, garlic, parsley, salt, sage and ½ tsp. ground black pepper. Mix well with the meat. Shape mixture into a loaf using a shallow baking pan. Bake at 350°F for 50 minutes. Drain off the fat.

Combine ketchup, sugar, and mustard, stir until smooth. Spread over meat. Return to oven for 10 minutes. Voilà!

"Real Meat" Loaf

Follow the preceding recipe but in place of the single ground chuck, make this adjustment:

    1 lb. ground chuck
    ½ lb. ground pork or pork sausage
    1 lb. ground veal

Mix the meats well and continue with recipe as above. This three-meat dish is very good, but can be expensive.

What good is comfort food without sugar? Here are two well-loved desserts that are too good for a dinner for two—you must share!

Peach Cobbler

    ½ c. + 2 Tbsp. brown sugar
    4 tsp. cornstarch
    ¼ tsp. ground mace or nutmeg
    ½ c. water
    4 c. fresh sliced peaches
    1 Tbsp. lemon juice
    1 Tbsp. butter or margarine
    biscuit dough or 1 can biscuits (enough for at least 4 biscuits)*

My mother knew I was not going to make biscuit dough, so she instructed me to use commercial biscuits: slice them in half horizontally and cover the fruit mixture with biscuits.

Combine ½ c. brown sugar, cornstarch, mace or nutmeg, and water in a saucepan. Cook, stirring until thickened and bubbly. Add peaches, lemon juice, and butter or margarine. Heat through. Stir biscuit dough, if using homemade dough. Pour hot fruit mixture into baking dish and place biscuit dough (homemade or from a can) on top of mixture. If using canned biscuits, place close together so that they are touching. Sprinkle 2 Tbsp. brown sugar on top of the dough or biscuits. Bake at 400°F for about 25 minutes. As the biscuits bake they will rise and spread, forming a crust.

Blessed are those who mourn, for they will be comforted.
—Matthew 5:4 (NIV)

Banana Pudding

1 c. + 2 Tbsp. sugar
¼ c. flour
pinch salt
4 c. milk
8 eggs, yolks and whites separated
1 Tbsp. vanilla
1 12-oz. box vanilla wafers
8 bananas, sliced

Custard:

Mix together 1 c. sugar, the flour, and the salt in a bowl. Pour the milk into a heavy saucepan and add the flour mixture. Heat. In a separate container, beat the egg yolks. Pour some of the hot milk mixture into the egg yolks and beat briefly.* Add the egg/milk mixture to the saucepan (with the milk and flour). Bring slowly to a boil, stirring constantly. Cook until thick enough to coat the back of a wooden spoon. Add the vanilla. Remove from heat and cover with plastic wrap to prevent a skin from forming on top. The plastic wrap should lie on top of the mixture, touching the entire surface.

Line the bottom and sides of a 9½" x 12½" baking pan (or other deep pan) with vanilla wafers. Add a layer of bananas, then another layer of vanilla wafers, alternating until all the bananas and wafers are used. Pour in the custard, completely covering the bananas and wafers.

Beat the egg whites until they form soft peaks. Add 2 Tbsp. sugar and beat until stiff, creating meringue. Spread the meringue over the pudding and bake at 375°F **until the meringue is golden** for 15–20 minutes.

If you don't follow directions and add the eggs to the hot milk mixture, you will have a hot mess—a pot of cooked egg fragments. Remember:

> *Pour*
> *Into*
> *Eggs*

Rice Pudding

¾ c. long-grain rice

3 c. milk (skim or low-fat)

4 large eggs

1 c. sugar

½ tsp. vanilla

Blueberries (optional)

heavy cream

cinnamon

nutmeg

raisins

Bring the rice and 1½ c. milk to boil. Cover the pot and reduce to simmer, 15–20 minutes or until the water is completely absorbed. Set rice aside.

Mix the eggs, sugar, and remaining 1½ c. milk in a saucepan. Stirring constantly, cook the mixture over low-medium heat for 10 minutes or until the ingredients are thoroughly combined. Remove from heat and add the vanilla. Stir well.

Combine the rice and milk mixture and place in greased 2½-qt. casserole or soufflé pan. Bake uncovered at 350°F for 15 minutes, and then *stir the pudding thoroughly* to keep the rice from settling to the bottom. Bake for 1 hour more, or until the top is light brown and somewhat shiny. The pudding will start to pull away very slightly from the sides of the casserole. Serve warm or cold with berries and a little cream.

The problem (and the joke)

That is the rice-pudding recipe in my mother's box—but the truth is, my mother would *never* cook rice to make a pudding. Instead she would use leftover rice, and we always had leftover rice. My grandmother used to say, "We eat more rice than all of China!"

My mother would slowly heat the leftover cooked rice in the eggs, sugar, and milk and proceed with her recipe. A generous portion of raisins would be added, along with nutmeg (to taste) and about ¼ tsp. cornstarch to thicken the mixture. Warm or cold, rice pudding was always good. Sprinkle a little cinnamon on top of warm pudding and serve. Rice pudding is the best solution for too much leftover rice!

Cake is the ultimate comfort food. Whether it is served with ice cream, a sauce drizzled over it, a cup of coffee, fresh fruit on top, a three-inch frosting, or just plain, a good cake will comfort any soul.

Baking Tip: Use a nonstick cooking spray to oil the surface of the cake pan. Dust the sprayed surface with cake flour; this prevents sticking and helps the cake leave the pan.

Two-Color Pound Cake

½ lb. butter

2 c. sugar

5 eggs

1 c. sour cream

1½ tsp. vanilla

3 c. flour, sifted

¼ tsp. baking soda

¼ tsp. salt

1 1-oz. square unsweetened chocolate, melted

1 Tbsp. hot water

1 Tbsp. sugar

Use a hand mixer and cream (or mix at high speed) butter and sugar until fluffy. Add eggs, one at a time, beating thoroughly after each addition. Blend in sour cream and vanilla. Sift flour, baking soda, and salt together. Gradually add dry mixture to creamed mixture; beat until blended smooth.

Divide batter into two parts. Mix 1 chocolate square, 1 Tbsp. water, 1 Tbsp. sugar, and ¼ tsp. baking soda and fold into half the batter. Alternately add spoonfuls of each batter into a 10" greased and floured tube pan. Bake at 350°F for 1 hour or until cake is done.

Pudding Cake

2 c. flour

1½ c. sugar

1 Tbsp. baking powder

¾ tsp. salt

10 Tbsp. shortening: solid, flavorless, veggie*

1 pkg. (almost 4 oz.) instant vanilla pudding mix

¼ c. vegetable oil

1 c. milk

1 tsp. vanilla

4 eggs

Sift together flour, sugar, baking powder, and salt. Cut in shortening until mixture forms very fine crumbs. Beat with electric mixer at low speed. Add pudding mix, oil, milk, and vanilla. Beat at high speed, (about 2 minutes), until smooth and creamy.

Add eggs and beat two minutes, until nice and creamy. Pour into greased and floured Bundt pan. Bake in a pre heated 350°F oven for 1 hour.

If using a 13x9 inch pan, bake for 40 minutes or until done. Test for done by inserting a toothpick or long skewer into the cake's center. If wood come out of the center clean, the cake is done.

Butter-Marshmallow Frosting

2/3 c. milk
32 large marshmallows
¾ c. (1½ sticks) butter
1 tsp. vanilla

Combine marshmallows and milk. Cook over low heat, stirring constantly until marshmallows dissolve. Cool to room temperature and stir to blend thoroughly. In a mixing bowl, cream butter until light and fluffy. Gradually add marshmallow mixture. Add vanilla. Makes enough to frost an 8" or 9" two-layer cake.

Cream Cheese Frosting

½ c. soft butter or margarine
1 8-oz. pkg. cream cheese, soft
1 tsp. vanilla extract
1 1-lb. box confectioners' sugar

Cream butter and cream cheese until light. Add vanilla. Slowly add sugar and beat until smooth. Makes 1½ cups.

Raspberry Sauce

1 12-oz. pkg. raspberries, without syrup
¾ c. sugar
1 tsp. lemon juice

Press raspberries through a strainer to remove seeds. Discard seeds. Combine the raspberry puree, sugar, and lemon juice. Blend well.

Bring mixture to a boil over medium heat. Boil 3 minutes, stirring constantly. Cool. Drizzle sauce over a slice of your favorite cake.

Caramel Sauce for Ice Cream or Cake

　　2 Tbsp. butter
　　1¼ c. brown sugar, firmly packed
　　2 Tbsp. dark corn syrup
　　½ c. half-and-half
　　½ tsp. vanilla

Melt butter. Add brown sugar and corn syrup. Stir and cook over medium heat, 1 minute. Remove from heat and add half-and-half. Cook and stir until sugar is dissolved, then simmer another minute. Remove from heat and add vanilla. Cool. The sauce should be thin enough to drizzle. If necessary, dilute with more half-and-half.

Is it a dessert or is it a vegetable? Is it a snack or is it an entrée?

The sweet potato is a starchy vegetable grown in warm climates. It is full of fiber and natural sugar. Although it's commonly eaten in America with sugar, molasses, or syrup added, the sweet potato can be enjoyed as a simple oven-baked snack, perhaps served with melted butter or margarine. The sweet potato is a diabetic's friend: a complex carbohydrate (so it fulfills sugar cravings) that contains protein, iron, vitamins A and C, calcium, and potassium. Bake it to retain its nutrients; boil it to peel and prepare the following sweet-potato dishes.

To prepare a nice, smooth sweet-potato pie or casserole, I highly recommend using a potato ricer and removing the fibrous strings found inside the sweet potato.

Choose long, red sweet potatoes from the produce section of your grocery store or from a farmers' market. They will produce a smooth texture and a naturally sweet taste.

Obtain a potato ricer from the cooking-utensil section of a department store or a cooking-supply store.

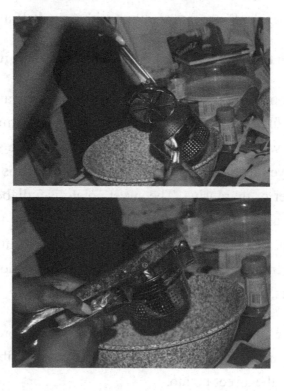

Boil your sweet potatoes until they are done. You'll know they're done when a fork or knife blade goes through the center of the potato with ease.

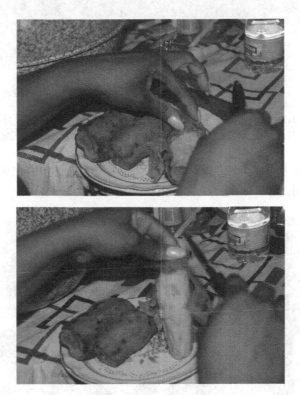

Open the ricer and place the potato (or half the potato, as necessary to fit) inside.

Squeeze the potato ricer shut. Everything that goes through the holes can be used.

Remove whatever remains in the ricer basket and discard. These are fibers.

Repeat the process for each cooked sweet potato.

Your dish will be better without the fibrous stings. These fibers are the material that resembles a sheet or a piece of sweet potato, clings to the back of the ricer, or can be picked up with your fork.

Now you are ready to create a smooth, delicious dish from the great sweet potato. Rice 3 or 4 boiled potatoes, and season to taste with butter, allspice, nutmeg, and brown sugar. Use a hand mixer and beat until smooth. Serve, or pour into a pie shell or pan and bake. Makes a quick, great side dish!

To use a sweet potato as a baked-potato side, simply scrub, dry, and oil the potato and bake at 350 for 30 minutes or until soft. Or bake a few and snack on them instead of potato chips.

My family kept sweet potatoes and served them boiled and mashed for impromptu meals. Just as mashed potatoes can accompany many different meals, we ate sweet potatoes with many meals.

Sweet-Potato Casserole

> 3 lbs. canned sweet potatoes or 3 –4 medium-sized fresh sweet potatoes
> ¾ c. orange juice
> 2 large eggs
> 2 Tbsp. melted butter
> 2 Tbsp. sugar
> 1½ tsp. cinnamon
> ½ tsp. nutmeg
> salt and pepper to taste

Topping

½ c. flour

¼ c. + 2 Tbsp. brown sugar

½ tsp. cinnamon

¼ cup butter

½ c. pecans

Grease an 8" baking dish. If using fresh sweet potatoes, boil until soft, peel, and mash. Add orange juice, eggs, butter, sugar, cinnamon, and nutmeg to the sweet potatoes. Beat until smooth. Season to taste with salt and pepper. Spoon mixture into baking dish.

For the topping, combine flour, brown sugar, and cinnamon. Cut in butter. Mix in pecans. Sprinkle topping over sweet potatoes.

Bake at 350°F for 30 minutes. Delicious with or without the topping!

> *For the Lord hath comforted his people, and will have mercy*
> *upon his afflicted.*
> *—Isaiah 49:13 (KJV)*

Walnut Sweet-Potato Pie

1 lb. sweet potatoes (about 3 medium), cooked and peeled

½ c. butter or margarine

1 14-oz. can sweetened condensed milk

1 tsp. grated orange rind

1 tsp. cinnamon

1 tsp. nutmeg

1 tsp. salt

2 eggs
1 9" unbaked pie shell

Walnut Topping

1 egg
3 Tbsp. dark corn syrup
3 Tbsp. light brown sugar, firmly packed
1 Tbsp. melted butter
½ tsp. maple flavoring
1 c. chopped walnuts

Beat hot sweet potatoes with butter or margarine until smooth. Add condensed milk and remaining ingredients, mix until a creamy consistency. Pour into pie shell. Bake at 350°F for 30 minutes.

While pie bakes, prepare Walnut Topping

Combine egg, corn syrup, 3 tbsp. firmly packed light brown sugar into spoon, melted butter and maple flavoring. Mix well. Stir in walnuts.

Remove pie from oven and spoon Walnut Toping over top. Bake 20–25 minutes longer, until golden brown. Serve warm or chilled.

> *Do you not know that your bodies are temples of the Holy Spirit, who is in you, whom you have received from God?*
> *—1 Corinthians 6:19 (NIV)*

Sweet-Potato Pie

4 medium sweet potatoes, enough to yield 2 c. mashed

1 unbaked 9" piecrust (or pie shell)

1 large egg white, beaten

1 stick (½ c.) butter or margarine, softened

2 large eggs

1¼ c. sugar

¼ c. milk

2 tsp. ground allspice*

1 tsp. pure vanilla extract**

Or try 1 tsp. allspice and 1 tsp. nutmeg
**Or try almond extract*

Boil unpeeled sweet potatoes on medium-high heat until they are soft, about 25 minutes. (Use a long fork to test for doneness; potatoes should be soft all the way through.) Prepare piecrust: prick all over with a fork, brush lightly with the beaten egg white, and set aside.

Drain potatoes and peel. I highly recommend using the procedure on the preceding pages, rice to remove strings. Transfer sweet potatoes to a bowl and beat on low speed until light and fluffy. Add butter or margarine, eggs, sugar, milk, allspice, and vanilla. Beat until filling is smooth and creamy, about 2–3 minutes.

Pour filling into piecrust, spread evenly. Place pie on bottom shelf of preheated 350°F oven; bake until lightly browned and a knife inserted into center comes out clean, about 1 hour. Cool on wire rack before serving.

That's a good recipe, but my mom and I always added nutmeg and a pinch of cinnamon. If you want to experiment with seasonings as we did, add in a little bit while you're beating the mixture, and then taste. What you taste is what you get: how the filling tastes at this stage is how the finished pie will taste. After your pie is done you can also add a meringue topping. Good luck, and enjoy a wonderful dessert!

My mom's best friend, Doris Williams, shared the following **Chess Pie** recipe with my mother. My mother used it often, and so I share it with you! It brings back good memories to me; we would sit and talk and eat this together.

Chess Pie

> 1 stick (1/2 c.) margarine
> 1½ cup sugar*
> 1½ tsp. self-rising cornmeal
> 1½ tsp. white vinegar
> 1 tsp. vanilla flavor
> 1 capful lemon juice or the juice of ½ a lemon
> dash allspice (optional)
> 5 eggs, lightly beaten
> 1 deep-dish piecrust

> *I think 1¼ c. is sufficient.*

Melt margarine combined with sugar over low heat until sugar dissolves then remove. Add all the other ingredients, adding the lightly beaten eggs last. Mix. Pour mixture into piecrust. Bake for a total of 45-60 minutes. Bake at 450°F for 15 minutes, lower heat to 300°F, and continue baking 30–45 minutes more. Pie is done when you insert a knife's blade into the center of the pie and the blade comes out clean. Pie should be golden brown.

> *You're blessed when you feel you've lost what is most dear to you. Only then can you be embraced by the One most dear to you.*
> —*Matthew 5:4 (The Message Bible)*

Relief Dough … Mad Ball … that's what my mother called dough for bread and rolls. Whenever you are mad, she taught me, go in the kitchen, gather your stuff, make a ball and *punch* it! Punch until you are exhausted; rest and punch again. When you are finished you'll have the lightest rolls. And the bread—like manna from heaven!

Baking bread and rolls is a great activity for relieving tension or anxiety. It produces a sense of calm, at least for me. I think it's a wonderful way to bond with children; my mother bonded with my daughter through the activity of preparing rolls.

Remove your rings and bracelets, put your hands in there, and play with that dough. *Knead* is a fancy word that means punch, roll, or manipulate the dough. The more my child, Precious, played in her dough, the lighter her rolls! They were always light and airy.

My mother had three methods she used to form rolls:

- Make three small balls of dough and place them in one muffin section.
- Roll the dough out into a two-inch-thick sheet and use a glass to cut out round shapes.
- Cut out triangles, start from the point, and roll them until a crescent is formed.

Always serve rolls warm, with soft butter. If there are leftovers, reheat them by putting them in a brown bag, wetting the bag on the outside, and placing in a 300°F oven for about 5 minutes. Now they are warmed and not burnt or dried-out.

You can brush the rolls with melted butter just before baking; this will help them reach a deep golden-brown color. You can also brush with egg yolk instead of butter; the egg yolk will give them a beautiful shine. But make your choice—golden brown or shiny—because you can only use one coating at a time.

> *Cast all your anxiety on him because he cares for you.*
> —1 Peter 5:7 (NIV)

Classic Dinner Rolls

2 pkgs. active dry yeast
½ c. warm water (105°–115°F)
1/3 c. sugar
¾ c. warm milk (105°–115°F)
1 tsp. salt
¼ c. (1/2 stick) butter, softened
5–5½ c. all-purpose flour
2 large eggs
melted butter to brush rolls

In a large bowl, sprinkle yeast over warm water. Add 1 Tbsp. of the sugar. Let stand until yeast is soft, about 5 minutes. Add remaining sugar, milk, salt, and butter. Add 2½ c. of the flour; beat on low speed until smooth and elastic, about 5 minutes.

Beat in eggs 1 at a time. Stir in by hand 2 c. more flour to make dough soft.

Turn dough onto lightly floured surface.

Knead, adding flour as needed until dough is smooth and satiny, 8–10 minutes.

Put dough in a large greased bowl. Turn to coat both sides. Cover with plastic wrap, then a towel. Let rise in warm place until the dough has doubled in bulk, about 1 hour, or refrigerate 6–8 hours.

Punch dough down; turn out onto lightly floured surface. Knead into a smooth ball. Cover with an inverted bowl; let rest 10 minutes. On lightly floured surface, shape dough into desired shape (for instance, 3 small balls together in muffin tin) and place on greased baking sheets. Cover rolls with plastic wrap and towel; let rise in warm place until almost doubled in size, 30–45 minutes, or refrigerate for 1 hour.

Brush rolls lightly with melted butter. Bake at 400°F until golden brown, 12–15 minutes. Cool slightly on wire racks. Serve warm. Makes 24 rolls.

PLATTERS AND PUNCH BOWLS

Go home and prepare a feast, holiday food and drink; and share it with those who don't have anything: This day is holy to God. Don't feel bad. The joy of God is your strength!
—Nehemiah 8:10 (The Message Bible)

Here is an assortment of treats to serve on a platter or in a punch bowl for holiday parties, a Super Bowl party, birthday celebrations, or the family movie. Carry a platter to an office party or place it on the TV table. Bring a punch bowl full of goodies to the next bridal or baby shower.

Potato Chip Cookies

1 lb. Imperial or Spry*
1 c. sugar
1 tsp. vanilla
¾ tsp. almond extract
3 c. flour
1 c. crushed potato chips

Imperial is margarine. Spry is shortening.

Cream margarine/shortening and sugar well. Add vanilla, almond extract, and flour; cream well. Mix in crushed potato chips. Drop 1 tsp. batter onto an ungreased cookie sheet. Bake at 350°F for 13–15 minutes. Makes about 100 cookies.

Bourbon Balls

3 c. (about 75) finely crushed vanilla wafers

2 c. powdered sugar

1 c. pecans, finely chopped*

¼ c. cocoa

½ c. bourbon**

¼ c. light corn syrup

granulated sugar, powdered sugar, or nuts, to coat balls

Or the nut of your choice.
**My mother used light Bacardi Rum to make this and called it Rum Balls.*

Mix crushed wafers, powered sugar, pecans, and cocoa. Stir in bourbon and corn syrup. Shape mixture into 1" balls. Roll balls in sugar or nuts. Refrigerate in a tightly covered container for several days before serving. Makes 5 dozen.

Note: Walnuts are a good source of omega-3 fatty acids, good for the heart, easy to find, and less expensive than pecans.

Punch-Bowl Cake

1 18.5-oz. pkg. yellow cake mix

2 (3 ½ -oz.) pkgs. instant vanilla pudding pie and filling

2 (8-oz.) cans crushed pineapple, undrained

2 (10-oz.) pkgs. frozen sliced strawberries, thawed

2 (8-oz.) containers frozen whipped topping, thawed

Maraschino cherries

chopped pecans*

Or the nut of your choice.

Prepare cake mix according to its directions; bake in two 8" or 9" cake pans; let cool. Prepare pudding according to its directions; set aside.

Crumble 1 cake layer into bottom of a large punch bowl. Spread half of the pudding over the cake. Top with 1 can pineapple with juice, 1 pkg. strawberries, and 1 container of whipped topping. Repeat layers with remaining cake, pudding, pineapple, strawberries, and whipped topping. Arrange cherries on top and sprinkle pecans over them. Chill overnight before serving. Makes 16 servings.

See the Punch Bowl Salad in the "Salad Bar" chapter.

Better Than Sex Cake

1 pkg. chocolate cake mix
12-oz. can sweetened condensed milk
12-oz. jar caramel topping
12-oz. container of whipped topping, or 12 oz. homemade whipped cream
3 Heath Bars, chopped up

Mix cake according to its directions; bake in a 9" x 13" pan. When cake is done, remove from oven and poke holes at random across entire cake with a fork. Spread the condensed milk over the cake, followed by the jar of caramel topping. Put cake back in the warm oven until caramel and milk have been absorbed. Remove and cool completely. Spread the whipped cream or topping over cake and sprinkle with Heath Bar pieces.

The Lord is my shepherd, I lack nothing.
Psalm 23:1 New International Version

Texas Sheet Cake

2 sticks (1 c.) margarine
1 c. water
4 Tbsp. cocoa
2 c. flour
2 c. sugar
½ tsp. salt
1 tsp. baking soda
2 eggs
1 c. sour cream (or 1 c. can milk with 1 Tbsp. of vinegar)

Icing

>1 stick (1/2 c.) margarine
>
>4 Tbsp. cocoa
>
>6 Tbsp. milk
>
>1 box powdered sugar
>
>1 tsp. vanilla
>
>1 c. nuts

Prepare Cake

Bring to boil 2 sticks margarine, 1 cup water, and 4 Tbsp. cocoa. Remove from heat and add 2 cups flour, 2 cups sugar, and ½ tsp. salt. Immediately beat in 1 tsp. soda, 2 eggs, and 1 cup sour cream (or milk and vinegar). Pour into a large greased cookie sheet. Bake at 375°F for 20–22 minutes.

While cake is baking, prepare icing.

Bring to boil 1 stick margarine, 4 Tbsp. cocoa, and 6 Tbsp. milk. Remove from heat and add 1 box powdered sugar, 1 tsp. vanilla, and 1 cup chopped nuts. Spread on cake as soon as it's removed from the oven.

White Texas Sheet Cake

>1 c. butter
>
>2 c. flour
>
>2 c. sugar
>
>2 eggs, beaten
>
>½ c. sour cream
>
>1 tsp. almond extract

1 tsp. salt

1 tsp. baking soda

Icing:

½ c. butter

¼ c. milk

4½ c. confectioners' sugar

½ tsp. almond extract

1 c. walnuts, chopped

Lightly grease a 10" x 15" x 1" jelly-roll pan and set aside. In a large saucepan over medium-high heat, bring butter and 1 c. water to a boil and remove from heat. With a wire whisk or wooden spoon, stir in flour, sugar, eggs, sour cream, almond extract, salt, and baking soda. Beat until smooth. Pour batter into prepared pan and bake at 375°F until center is done, about 25–30 minutes. Place pan on wire cooling rack.

Prepare icing: In a small saucepan over medium heat, combine butter and milk and bring to a boil. Remove from heat. Add confectioners' sugar and almond extract; mix well. Stir in walnuts and spread over warm cake. Let cool completely. Serves about 25.

In vain you rise early and stay late, toiling for food to eat-for he grants sleep to those he loves. Psalm 127:2 New International Version

Buttermilk Lemon Pound Cake

1½ c. flour

¼ tsp. baking soda

¼ tsp. baking powder

½ tsp. salt

½ c. butter at room temperature

1 c. sugar

2 eggs at room temperature

½ tsp. lemon extract

½ Tbsp. lemon rind

½ c. buttermilk

Sift together flour, baking soda, baking powder, and salt. Set aside.

Beat butter with an electric mixer until light. Add sugar and continue beating until light and fluffy. Add eggs all at once and beat until fluffy.

Spoon flour mixture into egg/butter/sugar mixture. Add lemon extract, lemon rind, and buttermilk. Mix batter with a wooden spoon until smooth; DO NOT BEAT. Pour into 2 greased and floured 7½" x 3½" loaf pans. Bake at 350°F until a toothpick inserted in center of loaf comes out clean, about 50–60 minutes. Makes 2 loaves, about 10–12 slices each.

The Lord is near to all who call on Him.
—Psalm 145:18 (NIV)

Pumpkin Bread

2 2/3 c. sugar

2/3 c. shortening

4 eggs beaten

1 (1-lb.) can pumpkin

2/3 c. water

3 1/3 c. flour, sifted

2 tsp. baking soda

½ baking powder

1½ tsp. salt

Whole grain and/or unbleached flour are better choices than white flour.

1 tsp. cinnamon

½ tsp. cloves

2/3 c. chopped nuts

2/3 c. dates, cut up

Cream together sugar and shortening until light and fluffy. Stir in eggs, pumpkin, and water. Sift together flour, baking powder, baking soda, salt, cinnamon, and cloves. Gradually stir dry ingredients into pumpkin mixture. Add nuts and dates; blend well.

Turn batter into 2 greased 9" x 5" x 3" pans. Bake at 350°F for about 1 hour and 15 minutes, or until done. Makes 2 loaves.

"If you hold on to me for dear life," says God, "I'll get you out of any trouble. I'll give you the best of care if you only get to know and trust me. Call me and I'll answer, be at your side in bad times; I'll rescue you, then throw you a party." Psalm 91:14-16 The Message

Do they still make punch bowls? Any party store will have beautiful clear bowls that serve the same purpose. Party stores have everything you need to make food pretty. Ceramic platters and glass or crystal punch bowls are beautiful and elegant to use and display in your home. However, if you are transporting food to be displayed and consumed elsewhere, party stores offer disposable platters that look like sterling silver, and plastic serving utensils that will be mistaken for real silverware.

It's important to present food that appeal to the eyes as well as making it as tasty as possible. Tricks to good food presentation are more valuable than gold for encouraging a grief-stricken person to eat.

- Surround baked fish or a whole chicken with uniform slices of orange, lime, or lemon. Choose one fruit or use all three for color and show.
- Cover the eye of a baked fish with a thin slice of olive or cherry tomato.
- Use fresh parsley and radishes to make "flowers."
- Make "flowers" from bay leaves and cherry tomatoes.
- Lay marinated shrimp or chicken on a bed of fresh, raw turnip greens. The greens will form little ruffles around the food.

Wikiwiki Punch for 16

3 6-oz. cans frozen lemonade concentrate
2 28-oz.bottles ginger ale
2 28-oz.bottles quinine water*
1 c. bottled grenadine syrup
ice or ice mold
½ lemon, sliced
½ lime, sliced
fresh mint

*My mother would never pay for water—"It comes out the faucet for free"—and we never used quinine water, also known as tonic water.

Ice Mold: The day before, fill a 6- to 8-cup Jell-O mold with water and freeze until firm. To remove, dip mold *very* quickly in and out of a pan of hot water; invert onto a plate and add ice mold to the punch. Have a little fun by adding food coloring to water in ice mold.

Punch: Combine lemonade concentrate, ginger ale, quinine water*, and grenadine syrup in a large bowl. Add a large ice mold or ice cubes. Thread lemon and lime slices with a sprig of mint; float mint on top.

It will come to you what to add to make this a Wicked Wicked Punch, which is what we really made. The original name is Quicky Quick Punch and was first made for my fifth birthday party, using tap water and juice. The recipe matured as I did; as time passed, we graduated from juice to … liquids a bit stronger.

Cast all your anxiety on him because he cares for you.
—1 Peter 5:7 (NIV)

Marinated Shrimp

1½ lbs. frozen shrimp, shelled and deveined
1/3 c. dry white wine
¼ c. pineapple juice
2 Tbsp. honey
2 Tbsp. soy sauce
1 Tbsp. lemon juice
1 clove garlic, crushed
½ tsp. ground ginger
dash cayenne pepper

While fresh shrimp are readily available, frozen shrimp are convenient. Thaw the shrimp by running cold water on them for five minutes. You will know they are thawed when they become flexible and easy to bend. Many packages have different cooking instructions. I prefer to put shrimp in a pot of heavily salted water and boil for 5 minutes. Another package may instruct you to sautee your shrimp in a pan of hot butter or hot oil until done. You will know the shrimp are done when they become an opaque pink with red tails. Do not overcook shrimp: they will dissolve.

Cook shrimp as directed on package; drain. Arrange shrimp in a single layer in an oblong baking dish, about 12" x 7½" x 2". Heat all other ingredients together until boiling. Reduce heat; simmer 5 minutes. Cool slightly and pour over shrimp. Cover and refrigerate at least 8 hours.

Remove shrimp from marinade with a slotted spoon; arrange on a serving platter on top of a bed of lettuce, or on top of fresh raw kale or raw turnip greens. My favorite is kale because it gives the appearence of shrimp lying on green ruffles. Serves 10-12 people

Why do people use the phrase, "Easy as pie"? A pie is not a simple dish—especially if it includes a meringue. If you do not beat the egg whites long enough, you'll have a runny mess. If you do not allow the mixture to cool, or if you pour eggs into the mixture instead of the mixture into the eggs, you will end up with cooked egg fragments floating in your pie filling. Take your time with this dish and you will have a beautiful, delicious showpiece to serve your guests (or yourself).

My mother edited her pie recipes just for me, because she knew I either could not or would not make a piecrust. She taught me how to use a store-bought piecrust. The pies in this collection do not require a top crust. Thanks, Mom!

> *Those who seek the Lord shall not lack any good thing.*
> *—Psalm 34:10 (Jubilee Bible)*

Lemon Meringue Pie

Pie

1½ c. sugar

1/8 tsp. salt

8 Tbsp. cornstarch

2 c. boiling water

¼ c. butter

grated rind of 1 lemon

½ c. lemon juice

3 eggs, separated (yolk from whites)

1 baked 9" pie shell

Meringue

1/8 tsp. salt

1 tsp. lemon juice

3 egg whites

6 Tbsp. sugar

Pie

Mix 1 ½ cup sugar, 1/8 tsp. salt, and cornstarch in a pot. Add the boiling water and 1 lemon rind. Cook until thickened, stirring, simmering, for 10 minutes. In a separate bowl, add lemon juice to egg yolks.

Remember PIE: **P**our **I**nto **E**gg

Slowly stir thickened sugar/cornstarch mixture into egg yolks. Strain into pie shell and bake in a preheated oven 400°F for 10 minutes.

Meringue

Add 1/8 salt and 1 tsp. lemon juice to egg whites; beat until firm. *Gradually* add 6 Tbsp. sugar and continue beating until very stiff. Pile meringue on pie and spread to edges. Reduce heat to 350°F and bake until gold or 18 minutes. Cool before slicing.

What is good food? To me, food is not good unless I am sharing or enjoying it with someone. What is comfort food? My definition of "comfort food" is something warm and thick (or both), tastes good and delivers happy thoughts and memories while consuming. It makes you sleepy soon after eating it. It takes your mind off of your troubles. Now comfort food is not the healthiest thing for the body; I don't recommend eating it every day, but it sure takes your mind off your woes when your mind is full of woe and trouble.

When I was a little girl food was used to comfort and console a troubled soul. It showed up at funerals. It was brought to the house of the sick and the sad. I remember seeing an older lady wrap a piece of homemade cake in a hankerchief and hand it to a younger lady just before she entered the church. I remember it as if it took place this morning; watching a grief stricken woman nibble pound cake at her 10 year old daughter's funeral. That slice of pound cake helped her maintain her composure during a time of grief and woe.

I have assembled here my mother's prized and most used recipes. She was a master at attending to one's soul through food.

Lillian took Jesus' instruction "Feed my sheep" seriously and fed anyone who said they were hungry. *Anyone*! Now you too can feed anyone by sharing what I've shared here—and you can help someone heal from grief by sharing the Soul Work Assignments.

Let all you do be done in love.
1 Corinthians 16:14 (New American Standard)

Do not forget that although you may have lost someone you deeply love, you are not alone, you are loved and you are needed. You may be experiencing a lost now, but take comfort in knowing that you had someone or something that once brought joy. The fact that you had any joy at all is a blessing.

You're blessed when you feel you've lost what is most dear to you. Only then can you be embraced by the One most dear to you. Psalm 5:4*

You're blessed when you've worked up a good appetite for God. He's food and drink in the best meal you'll ever eat. Psalm 5:6*

Let me tell you why you are here. You are here to be salt-seasoning that brings out the God-flavors of this earth. If you lose your saltiness, how will people taste godliness? Psalm 5:12*

*The Message (MSG), by Eugene H. Peterson

NOTES

NOTES

NOTES

NOTES

Printed in the United States
By Bookmasters